EXPOSED

The Hidden War of Love Spells & Witchcraft—Detect, Defy & Destroy for Victory

NONYE AKUBA

Although the publisher and the author have made every effort to ensure that the information in this book was correct at press time, and while this publication is designed to provide accurate information with regard to the subject matter covered, the publisher and the author assume no responsibility for errors, inaccuracies, omissions, or any other inconsistencies herein and hereby disclaim any liability to any party for any loss, damage, or disruption caused by errors or omissions, whether such errors or omissions result from negligence, accident, or any other cause.

The publisher and the author make no guarantees concerning the level of success you may experience by following the advice and strategies contained in this book, and you accept the risk that results will differ for each individual. The testimonials and examples provided in this book show exceptional results, which may not apply to the average reader, and are not intended to represent or guarantee that you will achieve the same or similar results.

The content of this book is for informational purposes only and is not intended to diagnose, treat, cure, or prevent any condition or disease. You understand that this book is not intended as a substitute for consultation with a licensed practitioner. Please consult with your own physician or healthcare specialist regarding the suggestions and recommendations made in this book. The use of this book implies your acceptance of this disclaimer.

Copyright @ 2025 by Nonye Akuba

All rights reserved. No part of this publication may be reproduced, distributed, or transmitted in any form or by any means, including photocopying, recording, or other electronic or mechanical methods, without the prior written permission of the author, except in the case of brief quotations embodied in critical reviews and certain other noncommercial uses permitted by copyright.

Abbreviation Key

AMP – The Amplified Bible
ESV – English Standard Version
ISV – International Standard Version
KJV – King James Version
NAB – New American Bible
NKJV – New King James Version
NLV – New Life Bible
NLT – New Living Translation
NRSV – New Revised Standard Version
TLV – Tree of Life Version
WEB – World English Bible

Anointed Hustle Books/The House of Noa Media Trade Paperback
ISBN: 978-1-7334793-9-4
Book Cover and Interior design by Anointing Productions

Published in the United States of America

*"Surely there is no enchantment against Jacob,
neither is there any divination against Israel."*

Numbers 23:23

Table of Contents

Introduction............................... 1

Chapter 1: In the Still of the Shadows............ 5

Chapter 2: Forbidden Power................... 9

Chapter 3: Discernment and Dominion.......... 41

Chapter 4: Witchcraft's Vessel: Architect of
                  Deception and Demonic Assault....... 51

Chapter 5: Freedom in Christ................. 61

Introduction

Is it just me, or does it seem like idolatry, blatant devil worship, and witchcraft are more prevalent and boldly unapologetic than ever before? A simple scroll on social media may have you encountering reels showcasing entertainers adorned with satanic symbols on their clothing and throughout their performances. Or maybe you'll discover, as I did, that one of your favorite actors summoned the devil to assist him with the execution of the role that introduced him to the masses and would further launch his burgeoning stardom. Even more likely may be a light-hearted curiosity to read an interview snippet from your favorite influencer that became an unwanted encounter with a story detailing a celebrity's use of witchcraft to cajole their mate into a love affair or marriage.

Whatever your experience with witchcraft's growing influence, heaven is sounding the alarm that it is urgent for believers to prioritize their understanding of spiritual matters in order to protect ourselves against the torrent of darkness hellbent on ushering in the emergence of a world devoid of the one true living God. If the title of this book has caught your attention, you may have a sincere desire to proactively protect yourself from falling victim to this attempt or from any encounters with a person(s) dabbling or fully entrenched in the demonic. You may be currently enmeshed in a relationship where you believe a spouse, mate, love interest, or friend has utilized witchcraft to successfully court, seduce, entrance and/or lead you into covenant with them. Regardless of your purpose for purchasing this book, this short read is geared to inform you on how to identify,

Introduction

counter, and disarm the use of witchcraft against your life. It can serve as a guide to detect witchcraft—when it is looming, present, or when you are under an all-out assault—and share how to escape. If you are the perpetrator of witchcraft, have been in the past, or paid someone else to engage in witchcraft on your behalf, knowingly or unknowingly, my prayer is that you would sincerely and wholeheartedly repent in the mighty, matchless, majestic, victorious, glorious, all-powerful, unshakeable, unbreakable name of our Lord and Savior, Jesus the Christ. Plead His blood over your past, present, and future, partake in communion often, and never engage again.

Hosea 4:6 KJV
"My people are destroyed for lack of knowledge."

I Corinthians 10:21 NKJV
"You cannot drink the cup of the Lord and the cup of demons too; you cannot have a part in both the Lord's table and the table of demons."

John 8:36 NKJV
"Therefore if the Son makes you free, you shall be free indeed."

If I were you, I would want to know why a person might believe they possess the expertise to author a book of this kind. And to be honest, it is a great question, as I am just a regular uptown New York—the Bronx, specifically—girl who grew up loving hip-hop, roller-skating, attending basketball games (yes including Harlem's own Rutger summer tournament), listening to mixtapes, and enjoying parties—lots of parties. I earned a Bachelor of Arts in English from Spelman College in Atlanta, Georgia, and a Master of Science in Management with a concentration in Strategy & Leadership at New York

Exposed

University's School of Professional Studies. No, I am not an ordained minister, and I have not attended seminary. Yet, I have experienced a unique and oddly peculiar three-year relationship with a man whom I would now deem an undercover warlock. This experience not only personally introduced me to witchcraft but revealed my identity and unique calling as a prophetic scribe: a calling that encompasses sharing my testimony as a blood-bought follower of Yeshua HaMashiach, Jesus the Christ, teaching others what I have been taught, and walking with Him in love, faith, authority, and power—not perfectly but authentically.

I have not been called to write this book to condemn, shame, or slander anyone. Yet, I will use my own testimony, spiritual experiences, and encounters, along with those of others to educate the naïve and unaware, illuminate darkness and hidden places of cruelty, and inspire the reader to flee from witchcraft and the many forms it takes—which include, but is not limited to santeria, juju, obeah, root work, voodoo, manipulation, and praying against the innocent. Whether you choose to believe it or not, there are many people in this world that resort to unscrupulous means to hurt, harm, deceive, control, and exact vengeance on others. Still others do inconceivable things to secure protection or to prove their loyalty or establish camaraderie with certain groups and affiliations. And so, whether you are the perpetrator of witchcraft or the victim, whether you engage in its use knowingly or unknowingly, my sincere prayer is that this book encourages and inspires your wholehearted decision to break free of it immediately and permanently.

John 3:16–21 NKJV
"For God so loved the world that He gave His only begotten Son, that whoever believes in Him should not

Introduction

perish but have everlasting life. For God did not send His Son into the world to condemn the world, but that the world through Him might be saved. He who believes in Him is not condemned; but he who does not believe is condemned already, because he has not believed in the name of the only begotten Son of God. And this is the condemnation, that the light has come into the world, and men loved darkness rather than light, because their deeds were evil. For everyone practicing evil hates the light and does not come to the light, lest his deeds should be exposed. But he who does the truth comes to the light, that his deeds may be clearly seen, that they have been done in God."

Psalm 74:20 NKJV
"Have respect unto the covenant; for the dark places of the earth are full of the habitations of cruelty."

AMP
"Consider the covenant [you made with Abraham], for the dark places of the land are full of the habitations of violence."

NLT
"Remember your covenant promises, for the land is full of darkness and violence!"

CHAPTER 1
In the Still of the Shadows

Long ago, the mere mention of witchcraft evoked images of a feeble, wrinkled old woman, hunched over in a secluded forest, stirring a cauldron of newts, eyeballs, and other things too ghastly to imagine. Others, however, might picture half-nude nymphs—mythical and whimsical—dancing gallantly to protect the endearing creatures of the realm, thanks to our favorite fantasy novels portraying them as guardians of all that is good, nature, and white magic.

No wonder many people today believe that there is a "good" and acceptable side to the occult and a "bad" side—good witches and bad witches. Yet, to truly understand the magnitude of deception in taking that stance, and how one can unsuspectingly and unknowingly fall into occult practices, we must understand the definition of witchcraft and what it encompasses.

Google's AI asserts that witchcraft can be defined as "The use of spiritual means to manipulate circumstances, gain power, or obtain knowledge, typically by contacting and relying on demonic or spiritual forces other than God."

For the Christian, I would enhance this definition by stating witchcraft is the use of spiritual means, decrees, rituals, and actions to manipulate circumstances and outcomes, gain power, knowledge, wealth, connect with the spiritual plane, and/or curry favor, entrap, ostracize—and at times deliberately inflict harm unto death upon others—by contacting and relying on spiritual forces or entities (all demonic) other than God, the Father almighty, creator of heaven and earth, Jesus the Christ, His Son and the Holy Spirit, our Helper.

Google goes on to state that witchcraft primarily includes five practices. These practices are cited as sorcery, divination/fortune telling, necromancy (consulting the dead), casting spells, and pharmakeia (the use of mind-altering drugs to achieve altered states). I would even assert, with all diligence, that trying to achieve altered states via the auditory senses, like burning incense , can also be demonic in the wrong hands and with the wrong intentions.

Love spells fall under the umbrella of witchcraft and involve the casting of a spell. I define a love spell as any chant, incantation, affirmation, or action done (singularly, in repetition, and/or stealth) to curry favor or elicit an outcome, behavior, encounter, or most commonly to begin, maintain, or end a relationship with a romantic interest—the object of one's desire or a romantic rival—against the person's will and more specifically, against the will of God.

A love spell can also be utilized to create a state of ***spiritual bondage*** where the object is bound to the perpetrator mentally, physically, emotionally, or even financially. A love spell wielded in this manner can be initiated, sustained, and strengthened through one's looks, words, and through manipulation—mental, emotional, spiritual, and financial, as well as through sexual intercourse (within and outside of the covenant of marriage) or intimidation.

Ezekiel 13:20–21 AMP
"Therefore, thus says the Lord God, 'Behold, I am against your magic bands [and veils] by which you hunt [human] lives as birds and I will tear them from your arms; and I will let the lives you hunt go free, even those lives whom you hunt as birds. I will also tear off your [pagan] veils and rescue My people from your hands, and they will no longer be in your grip to be hunted and trapped. Then you will know [without any doubt] that I am the Lord.'"

CHAPTER 2
Forbidden Power

Many people believe casting love spells is no big deal, maybe even inconsequential, a means to an end. Just a harmless method by which they can seduce the love of their life. Others believe casting a spell is simply an extension of manifesting, akin to utilizing visualization techniques. (As a Christian, I would argue that the practices of manifesting your intentions and the use of visualization techniques outside of total submission to the will of God and lordship of Yeshua HaMashiach are risky undertakings. To be blunt, it is witchcraft.) Truthfully, these practices and behaviors are far more sinister and perilous than we can ever imagine, as they open portals and doors that invite spirits, beings, powers, and principalities that pale in comparison to our scariest nightmares or any movie we have ever seen—and often there are deadly consequences. When a person seeks to influence a romantic interest to respond to them favorably by repeating chants, or by the use of sensual and intimately masterful prowess in the bedroom (making love to their minds), or when one seeks to gain an edge over romantic rivals by using psychics, fortune tellers, zodiac charts, horoscope readings, and/or tarot cards to peer into the activities, love life, or desires of their mate, that person is utilizing witchcraft. And according to the Bible, they are guilty of rebellion against God. For God is not the spirit, nor power, behind these occult practices.

If indeed our Father, God the Father, creator of heaven and earth is omniscient, omnipresent, and omnipotent (in other words, if we truly believe He is all-knowing, all-powerful, all-seeing, all-righteous, all-sustaining, all-sufficient, and all sovereign), and we are instructed to seek Him and His will in all matters, situations, trials, and aspects of daily life…if it is true that He knows what we need before we ask—and even more miraculously, He answers before we ask—then witchcraft is the epitome of operating in our own wills and is blatantly against His authority.

Isaiah 46:10 NLT
"Only I can tell you the future before it even happens. Everything I plan will come to pass, for I do whatever I wish."

Isaiah 65:24 NKJV
"It shall come to pass That before they call, I will answer; And while they are still speaking, I will hear."

Matthew 6:8 NKJV
"Therefore do not be like them. For your Father knows the things you have need of before you ask Him."

Jeremiah 23:24 NKJV
"'Can anyone hide himself in secret places, So I shall not see him?' says the Lord; 'Do I not fill heaven and earth?' says the Lord."

Psalm 139:7–10 NKJV
"Where can I go from Your Spirit? Or where can I flee from Your presence? If I ascend into heaven, You are there; If I make my bed in hell, behold, You are there. If I take the wings of the morning, And dwell in the uttermost

parts of the sea, even there Your hand shall lead me, and Your right hand shall hold me."

Deuteronomy 18:10–12 NKJV
"There shall not be found among you anyone who makes his son or daughter pass through the fire [as a sacrifice], one who uses divination and fortune-telling, one who practices witchcraft, or one who interprets omens, or a sorcerer, or one who casts a charm or spell, or a medium, or a spiritist, or a necromancer [who seeks the dead]. For everyone who does these things is utterly repulsive to the Lord; and because of these detestable practices the Lord your God is driving them out before you."

Leviticus 19:31 AMP
"Do not turn to mediums [who pretend to consult the dead] or to spiritists [who have spirits of divination]; do not seek them out to be defiled by them. I am the Lord your God."

I have encountered people who choose to worship what they believe are African gods, ancestral deities, or even their forefathers, claiming these beings are more aligned with their heritage and spiritual roots. Yet petitioning ancestors for guidance or help—whether in love, life, or in any area—is still witchcraft, idolatry, and an abomination to the Lord.

In the New Testament, Jesus tells the young man who wished to bury his father before following Him to "let the dead bury their own dead," not because He dismisses grief or dishonoring one's parents, but to teach that our focus belongs on God, and the purpose He endows all of us with. It demonstrates how the concerns of this world can distract us from what is most important to the Lord, which is the living and the mission to spread the Gospel. It does not directly speak to seeking the counsel, involvement, or intervention of those who have passed on, but we can use it to shed light on Jesus's sentiment regarding prioritizing the dead.

Luke 9:60 NKJV
"Jesus said to him, 'Let the dead bury their own dead, but you go and preach the kingdom of God.'"

The Old Testament shows the danger of seeking the dead through the account of Saul and the witch of Endor after the prophet Samuel's death. After previously driving out witches, sorcerers, and all who practiced the occult from Israel, Saul—desperate to hear from the Lord through Samuel — went secretly to consult a medium because God no longer answered him through prayer, prophets, or dreams. Even then, the Lord did not respond to him. Instead, Samuel appeared and rebuked him, saying, "Why have you disquieted me?" His irritation, mild indignation, suggests that his peace was disturbed and reveals that the dead are not meant to be summoned or relied upon. Saul's obsession to hear from Samuel illustrates a lack of trust in God and dependence on men, which drive many of us to engage in practices that dishonor the Lord.

If consulting the dead were acceptable, Saul would not have expelled occult practitioners, nor would he have disguised himself to seek the medium's help. His secrecy and Samuel's rebuke are evidence that such practices are forbidden and displeasing to God.

Isaiah 8:19 AMP
"When the people [instead of trusting God] say to you, 'Consult the mediums [who try to talk to the dead] and the soothsayers who chirp and whisper and mutter,' should not a people consult their God? Should they consult the

dead on behalf of the living?"

1 Samuel 28:3 AMP
"Now Samuel had died, and all Israel had mourned for him and buried him in Ramah, his own city. And Saul had removed the mediums and the spiritists (soothsayers) from the land."

1 Samuel 28:6
"And when Saul inquired of the LORD, the LORD answered him not, neither by dreams, nor by Urim, nor by prophets."

I Samuel 28:8 AMP
"So Saul disguised himself by wearing different clothes, and he left with two men, and they came to the woman at night. He said to her, 'Conjure up for me, please, and bring up [from the dead] for me [the spirit] whom I shall name to you.'"

1 Samuel 28:15 KJV
"And Samuel said to Saul, 'Why hast thou disquieted me, to bring me up?'"

Ecclesiastes 9:5–6 NKJV
"For the living know that they will die; but the dead know nothing, and they have no more reward,

For the memory of them is forgotten. Also their love, their hatred, and their envy have now perished;

Nevermore will they have a share in anything done under the sun."

When we refuse to rely on God, it is the pinnacle of mistrust, and it is rebellion against His very nature and our design as His children. It is the ultimate violation of how we are instructed to interact with Him; it is the ultimate betrayal—pure rebellion. And one's refusal to stop easily morphs into stubbornness and sets one's commitment to these practices above God—which is idolatry.

1 Samuel 15:23 KJV
"For rebellion *is as* the sin of witchcraft, and stubbornness *is as* iniquity and idolatry. "

As cited earlier, Google AI rightfully identifies witchcraft as idolatry and rebellion. What many people have for centuries peddled as harmless spells, charms, techniques, and the womanly arts to lure the love of their lives is—if we are indeed instructed to solely rely upon the Word of God as a guide for our daily lives—witchcraft, period.

What truly falls under the auspice of witchcraft in this sense? Well, it would be the myriad practices that hinge upon deceptive means, many of which are totally obvious even to those that do not consider themselves believers or spiritual. Other practices can be normal, day-to-day activities that, when practiced with good intentions and outside of nefarious objectives, are widely acceptable, welcomed, and employed by the masses.

Surveillance

When considering witchcraft, surveillance can take many forms. I am not speaking of surveillance utilized by law enforcement for the purposes of intelligence, security, and preventing harm, or even of spiritual oversight by God's watchers and angelic beings. Surveillance in a demonic sense can range from utilizing psychics and fortune tellers, stalking, the use of audio and visual means to record, spy on, or listen to the conversations, private moments, and lives of unsuspecting victims. For instance, watching someone in the privacy of their home, unbeknownst to them, or leaving a recording device in the home or vehicle of a loved one to be privy to information you would not normally hear or know to influence their decisions, actions, and/or feelings toward you, is willful distrust of God and is witchcraft. Surveillance efforts targeting another's social media accounts (whether private or public) can be considered demonic as well if the watcher's intentions are villainous.

Hebrew 4:13 NKJV
"But all things are naked and open to the eyes of Him to whom we must give account."

Ecclesiastes 12:14 NIV
"For God will bring every deed into judgment, including every hidden thing, whether it is good or evil."

Psalm 101:7 NIV
"No one who practices deceit shall dwell in my house…"

Luke 8:17 WEB
"For nothing is hidden that will not be revealed, nor anything secret that will not be known and come to light."

Dance
This one may seem strange, but have you ever watched a movie with a striptease scene when the person on the receiving end of the dance becomes absolutely mesmerized? Even to the point of parting with all of their money and resources? Don't believe me? Was it not Herodias' daughter's dance that so captivated King Herod he consented to deliver the head of John the Baptist? I love to dance, and I have been known to cut a rug or two. There is absolutely nothing wrong with heading to the dance floor to enjoy your favorite songs,

being a dancer of the arts, or watching dance performances. Yet when dance is utilized as a means to seduce, entrap, or influence one to part from their resources, reason, logic, or dull their mental faculties—that is a form of witchcraft.

Mark 6:22–24 AMP
"Now [Salome] the daughter of Herodias came in and danced [for the men]. She pleased *and* beguiled Herod and his dinner guests; and the king said to the girl, 'Ask me for whatever you want and I will give it to you.' And he swore to her, 'Whatever you ask me, I will give it to you; up to half of my kingdom.' She went out and said to her mother, 'What shall I ask for?' And Herodias replied, 'The head of John the Baptist!'"

Music

You may believe citing music as a means of witchcraft is a stretch. Yet, if music is utilized to praise, honor, and worship the Lord, a logical deduction would be that it could be utilized for opposing purposes. As children, we were taught about a legendary folk hero or villain—depending on how you view the story—who was hired to magically lure rodents away from a German town. Yet, when the townspeople failed to pay him for his work, he returned and lured the townspeople's children away in the same manner. There are many versions of the story's ending, the morals of which are not the purpose of its citing here. But I mention it to demonstrate the accepted wisdom of the power of music to influence and inspire allegiance and loyalty. If David's harp soothed King Saul and drove out the demonic spirit tormenting him, is it so far-fetched to assert that music can be used to welcome one? Many music industry executives have come forward and gone on record to state they have witnessed or participated in chants, spells, and rituals performed for and over their artists' music to inspire sales via loyalty to the song or artist, or even more insidiously, to program the masses and entrap them into demonic covenants.

I am by no means prepared to write a dissertation on this topic, but I am called to share what I have learned, present the idea, and hopefully spark some understanding. Many thought leaders suggest that certain types of music emit frequencies that can influence or even encourage negative atmospheres and behaviors. As someone who genuinely loves hip-hop music, I have to be honest: When I consider the violent content found in much of today's hip-hop lyrics, alongside the rising murder rates among our young people, I can't help but believe that music plays a significant role.

I cannot state that music has been utilized to bewitch me in a romantic sense. Like many of you, I have received a song or two from a love interest to express their intentions or feelings to substitute for their expressive limitations, and I have known a few girlfriends that have sent cassettes to boyfriends to express discontent over a break-up, etc. I hope that the intentions behind these actions were innocent and meant to evoke common ground and understanding. Could their objectives have been more sinister? Anything is possible, but I do not believe that was the case. Although Christians should remain vigilant in knowing that music, more specifically, the playing of certain songs by a romantic interest, who may not be as sincere as they propose, can be used to deceive, manipulate, and relax boundaries. Music is transformative and is a powerful tool. In the right hands, it can be wielded for worship of our Lord, healing, upliftment, inspiration, love, joy, hope, and camaraderie. In the wrong hands, it has the power to cause damage; spread lies, trauma, hate, and misinformation; and influence negative emotions, actions, and social movements.

1 Samuel 16:14–23 AMP
"Now the Spirit of the Lord departed from Saul, and an evil spirit from the Lord tormented *and* terrified him. Saul's servants said to him, 'Behold, an evil spirit from God is tormenting you. Let our lord now command your servants who are here before you to find a man who plays skillfully on the harp; and when the evil spirit from God is on you, he shall play *the harp* with his hand, and you will be well.' So Saul told his servants, 'Find me a man who plays well and bring him to me.' One of the young men said, 'Behold, I have seen a son of Jesse the Bethlehemite who is a skillful musician, a brave *and* competent man, a warrior, discerning (prudent, eloquent) in speech, and a handsome man; and the Lord is with him.' So Saul sent messengers to Jesse and said, 'Send me David your son, who is with the flock.' Jesse took a donkey [loaded with] bread and a jug of wine and a young goat, and sent them to Saul with David his son. Then David came to Saul and attended him. Saul loved him greatly and [later] David became his armor bearer. Saul sent *word* to Jesse, saying, 'Please let David be my attendant, for he has found favor in my sight.' So it came about that whenever the [evil] spirit from God was on Saul, David took a harp and played it with his hand; so Saul would be refreshed and be well, and the evil spirit would leave him."

Sexual Hypnosis/Intoxication

When considering sexual hypnosis, I am not referring to any medical or psychological practices coined by practitioners or mental health scholars that suggest the integration of hypnosis with sexual intercourse. Nor am I referring to any erotic role-playing practices under the umbrella of bondage, discipline, dominance, submission, sadomasochism or the like. What I am referencing here is of a spiritual nature. Although I would assert that sexual hypnosis and BDSM are both demonic in nature, for the purposes of this guide, I would like to focus on what is mentioned in social circles in jest, joked about in intimate settings between family and friends, loved ones, and elders. In the Black community it is often called being "whipped," and it typically points to a lover's sexual prowess and skill in the bedroom to the extent that the lover on the receiving end enters a fog-like state, unable to make logical and/or reasonable decisions concerning their mate or the relationship. Ultimately, the lover enters a state of addiction and codependency. And it is no laughing matter—especially if the snare is calculated, intentional, utilized for gain of any kind and/or to keep their lover-turned-victim in bondage.

Jeremiah 5:26 KJV
"For among my people are found wicked men; they lay wait, as he that setteth snares; they set a trap, they catch men."

MSG
"My people are infiltrated by wicked men, unscrupulous men on the hunt. They set traps for the unsuspecting. Their victims are innocent men and women."

Psalm 140:5 NKJV
"The proud have hidden a snare for me, and cords; They have spread a net by the wayside; They have set traps for me."

Psalm 142:3 KJV
"… In the way wherein I walked have they privily laid a snare for me."

There are many renowned love stories in the Bible—Isaac and Rebekah (Genesis 24–27), Ruth and Boaz (Ruth 3–4), and even Jacob and Rachel (Genesis 28–30) remain among my favorites. Yet Scripture also offers numerous accounts—some subtle, some overt—that warn God's children about the dangers of choosing the wrong partners or spouses. These stories illustrate how easily the insidious, contagious, and seductive nature of witchcraft and ungodly influence can infiltrate a believer's life through unhealthy or spiritually misaligned relationships.

When an unsuspecting person engages in repeated sexual intercourse with a practitioner of sexual hypnosis or any form of witchcraft, they can begin to develop an affinity for whatever spiritual influences that practitioner is submitted to. If the practitioner engages in crystal healing or metaphysical religions, the love interest often drifts in that direction. If the practitioner relies on psychics, numerology, consults tarot cards, follows zodiac-based personality doctrines, or openly worships Satan, it becomes highly likely that their partner—apart from a genuine belief in and loyalty to Christ—will eventually succumb to that same belief system. Whether they adopt those practices fully or merge them into a hybrid belief system, the spiritual outcome remains the same: exposure to, and a growing allegiance toward, rebellion against God.

In this same manner, King Solomon—renowned for his wisdom, but also known for having seven hundred women as wives, princesses, and concubines—displeased the Lord, for these wives led him astray. When closely considering King Solomon's error, God's forewarning teaches us that He did not view these women as pious and upright. As such, are we to believe that each of them made King Solomon's acquaintance and then caught his eye and attention through just means?

Are we to believe that they only led King Solomon astray with their words? Or are we astute enough to deduce that there may have been other factors outside of their personalities, character, physical beauty, and potential to strengthen politically strategic alliances that led him to abandon his God? Is it really far-fetched to consider that many of them may have used spells, chants, rituals, or even forms of sexual hypnosis to influence him and secure his favor?

1 Kings 11:1–5 NKJV
"But King Solomon loved many foreign women, as well as the daughter of Pharaoh: women of the Moabites, Ammonites, Edomites, Sidonians, and Hittites—from the nations of whom the Lord had said to the children of Israel, 'You shall not intermarry with them, nor they with you. Surely they will turn away your hearts after their gods.' Solomon clung to these in love. And he had seven hundred wives, princesses, and three hundred concubines; and his wives turned away his heart. For it was so, when Solomon was old, that his wives turned his heart after other gods; and his heart was not loyal to the Lord his God, as was the heart of his father David."

The turning of King Solomon's heart toward these women does not only refer to turning to other gods but the exposure to and eventual intermingling—possibly dependence on—their practices. And if these practices were so ingrained in them that they would influence King Solomon to abandon his God, then it's probable that many utilized their witchcraft on him directly.

1 Kings 11:1–5 teaches us that Solomon's wives, princesses, and concubines included Moabites, Ammonites, Edomites, Sidonians, and Hittites—all of whom practiced witchcraft.

Each nation was identified by the Lord as practitioners of witchcraft in one form or another. Balak, the Moabite, asked Balaam, the false prophet, to curse the Israelites (Numbers 22:5–7). God judged the Ammonites for ripping developing fetuses out of the wombs of pregnant women to win battles, which suggests hellish, demonic rituals (Amos 1:13). Concerning the Edomites, before the Lord released His judgment on them, He jeered them about their wisdom—wisdom and knowledge they held in high esteem, even higher than the omniscience of God (Jeremiah 49:7). We learn that the infamous Jezebel, hunter of the prophets of God, was the daughter of the Sidonian King, and through her marriage to King Ahab she led Israel to practice idolatry and sorcery. We see this in the words of Jehu to her son, Joram, charging her with idolatry and witchcraft in 2 Kings 9:22. The Hittites were descendants of Heth, a son of Canaan, who is the father of the Canaanites. Both nations were descendants of Noah's son Ham. God instructed Israel to rid the promised land of pagans, which included several idolatrous nations—the Canaanites, the Hittites, and many others—and He specifically forbade them to take on their customs of witchcraft (Deuteronomy 18:9–12). Charging these women with witchcraft is not a matter I take lightly, yet I contest that it is both implied and explicitly stated in the Bible.

I would also assert that the love stories associated with Samson warrant a closer look. We know that Samson, although imbued with great purpose, struggled with lust. His desire to marry the Philistine woman from Timnah, although orchestrated by the Lord to bring judgment against the Philistines, vividly illustrates his propensity for fleshly temptations cloaked in beautiful women and, dare I say, an opportunity to satisfy his sexual appetite. So much so that his response to the warning of his parents not to marry a Philistine woman seems jarringly obstinate and bullheaded. I am not trying to give Samson a bad rap, nor am I being unjustly judgmental. I am utilizing the Word of God to illustrate a weakness that the Lord wants us to take note of, for if this were not the case, his next encounter with a woman would not have been with a prostitute from Gaza. There is no other reason mentioned regarding his purpose for entering the city other than to engage in that sexual encounter.

Soon after this, Samson meets Delilah. And here is where it gets deep—for he meets Delilah in the Valley of Sorek. Many pastors have delivered sermons based on the etymology of the word sorek and how its deeper meaning is woven into Samson's ultimate fall. A favorite of mine is a sermon by Pastor Mark Moore, Jr., of Spirit and Truth Church, entitled, "Pop the Balloon or Find God," where he brilliantly explains Samson's type of romantic partner and why it was toxic for his calling. It is here where I would like to direct our attention as Sorek is a Hebrew word defined in the Blue Letter Bible as "choice vine." Bible Hub's Topical Encyclopedia cites the etymology and location of the word as having a "historical association with vineyards and wine production," and its Lexical Summary notes it "yielded purple grapes, the richest variety." Yet, Samson was a Nazarite, one who specifically had taken a vow to be consecrated to God—that vow including abstaining from wine and alcohol. We all understand the intoxicating elements and outcomes of ingesting wine and alcohol. We can also agree that God is intentional and that He weaves, integrates, and intermingles the meaning of individuals, places, and events in ways that have profound meaning and revelation. Therefore, it is plausible that Delilah was not only toxic to Samson, as Pastor Moore suggests, but just as intoxicating as the place where she resided...a fleshly intoxication that encompassed and surpassed mere words.

Rituals
I would define a ritual as a behavior, action, ceremony, or the reciting of an oath in secrecy by an individual or a group to elicit a desired response. Desired responses can range from blind loyalty to harm, to create or strengthen a soul tie to facilitate the mental, emotional, spiritual, physical, and/or financial bondage of one individual to another person or group of people.

Rituals can range from the placing a stick of cinnamon inside a jar of honey in a hidden place or cabinet with the object of affection's name written on the jar, to human sacrifices, graveyard visitations, and clandestine outings to the woods to build altars with the intent of engaging spiritual entities that can inspire, enforce, and/or perpetuate servitude or adverse actions against the intended. Rituals include the stealing or harboring of an individual's photo to utilize as a point of contact that would bring about the person's harm, return, or communication. In recent days, we have witnessed humiliation rituals of all sorts and rituals performed that openly praise Satan and the demonic by entertainers in the music industry and beyond. My sister in Christ, Jenny Weaver (whom I do not know personally) has written a book, *The Wicked World of Witchcraft: Exposing the Rise of Darkness*, if you would like to explore this subject more in depth.

Isaiah 65:3–4 NLT
"All day long they insult me to my face by worshiping idols in their sacred gardens. They burn incense on pagan altars. At night they go out among the graves, worshiping

the dead. They eat the flesh of pigs and make stews with other forbidden foods."

1 Corinthians 10:20 NIV
"No, but the sacrifices of pagans are offered to demons, not to God, and I do not want you to be participants with demons."

Jeremiah 7:31 NKJV
"And they have built the high places of Tophet, which is in the Valley of the Son of Hinnom, to burn their sons and their daughters in the fire, which I did not command, nor did it come into My heart."

Psalm 106:37 NKJV
"They even sacrificed their sons and their daughters to demons."

Colossians 2:18 AMP
"Let no one defraud you of your prize [your freedom in Christ and your salvation] by insisting on mock humility and the worship of angels…"

Colossians 2:18–19 NAB
"Let no one disqualify you, delighting in self-abasement and worship of angels, taking his stand on visions, inflated without reason by his fleshly mind."

What the naïve and unassuming fail to recognize is that many of the demonic rituals in which they engage try to, but can never duplicate, replicate, or surpass the inherent power within the crucifixion and resurrection of Christ. For by His love for us, His sacrifice of His own life, His subjection to mockery and humiliation and triumph over death, He offered Himself as a ransom for our sins, taking on the penalty of sinful natures to reconcile us back to the love of God, the Father Almighty.

Isaiah 53:3–12 AMP
"He was despised and rejected by men, a Man of sorrows and pain and acquainted with grief; and like One from whom men hide their faces He was despised, and we did not appreciate His worth or esteem Him. But [in fact] He has borne our griefs, and He has carried our sorrows and pains;

Yet we [ignorantly] assumed that He was stricken, struck down by God and degraded and humiliated [by Him]. But He was wounded for our transgressions, He was crushed for our wickedness [our sin, our injustice, our wrongdoing]; the punishment [required] for our well-being fell on Him, and by His stripes (wounds) we are healed. All of us like sheep have gone astray, we have turned, each one, to his own way;

But the Lord has caused the wickedness of us all [our sin, our injustice, our wrongdoing] to fall on Him [instead of us]. He was oppressed and He was afflicted, yet He did not open His mouth [to complain or defend Himself]; like a lamb that is led to the slaughter, and like a sheep that is silent before her shearers,

So He did not open His mouth. After oppression and judgment He was taken away; and as for His generation [His contemporaries], who [among them] concerned himself with the fact that He was cut off from the land of the living [by His death] for the transgression of my people, to whom the stroke [of death] was due? His grave was assigned with the wicked, but He was with a rich man in His death, because He had done no violence, nor was there any deceit in His mouth. Yet the Lord was willing to crush Him, causing Him to suffer; If He would give Himself as a guilt offering [an atonement for sin], He shall see His [spiritual] offspring, He shall prolong His days, and the will (good pleasure) of the Lord shall succeed and prosper in His hand. As a result of the anguish of His soul, He shall see it and be satisfied; by His knowledge [of what He has accomplished] the Righteous One, My Servant, shall justify the many [making them righteous—upright before God, in right standing with Him], for He shall bear [the responsibility for] their sins. Therefore, I will divide and give Him a portion with the great [kings and rulers], and He shall divide the spoils with the mighty, because He [willingly] poured out His life to death, and was counted among the transgressors; yet He Himself bore and took away the sin of many, and interceded [with the Father] for the transgressors."

As such, the futile ploys to sacrifice human beings and animals to counter the power of Yeshua HaMashiach's sacrifice and His shed blood, the contrived humiliation rituals and the summoning of demons and the dead to overthrow the omniscient, omnipresent, and omnipotent power of God fail every time—miserably.

I John 1:7 NLT
"But if we are living in the light, as God is in the light, then we have fellowship with each other, and the blood of Jesus, his Son, cleanses us from all sin."

Hebrew 9:14 NIV
"How much more, then, will the blood of Christ, who through the eternal Spirit offered himself unblemished to

God, cleanse our consciences from acts that lead to death, so that we may serve the living God!"

Acts 20:28 AMP
"Take care and be on guard for yourselves and for the whole flock over which the Holy Spirit has appointed you as overseers, to shepherd (tend, feed, guide) the church of God which He bought with His own blood."

Blood and Potions

This is the sole reason why witches, warlocks, wizards, witch doctors, and the like fervently believe in and utilize blood in their rituals and for potions. It is not to suggest that all demonic potions require blood, but many do, as they believe it intensifies the power of their rituals. Yet, there is no blood sacrifice that can counter the potency and efficacy of the Blood of the Lamb that was slain before the foundations of the world (Revelation 13:8, Revelation 12:11).

I have heard, as have many of you reading this book, many instances of women secretly using blood from their menses in meals to secure a man's loyalty and "love." I have heard stories of people seeking the blood and body parts of infants to strengthen the might of their efforts. Survivors of satanic cults speak of pregnancies that are intentionally aborted for the blood and body parts of fetuses and newborn infants snuffed out for the same (see Pastor Dave Bryan's testimony).

As previously mentioned, these blood rituals are not new and were practiced in biblical times. The Ammonites sacrificed their children to appease and curry favor with their god, Molech (Jeremiah 32:35). King Manasseh (2 Chronicles 33:6, 2 Kings 21:6), King Ahaz (2 Chronicles:28), and Mesha of Moab (2 Kings 3:27), are cited in the Bible as participants

Exposed

in this detestably horrific practice—and each still lost the battles that ensued against their enemies.

Yet, potions do not always require blood for their use to be considered. Any use of a potion or elixir that is created, ingested, or applied with the intention of receiving a desired end outside of the will of God, or to circumvent His will or assistance, is demonic. I am not referring to acts of self-care that would include moisturizing oneself after bathing or when your skin is dry. Nor do I mean partaking of a healthy portion of your grandmother's delicious chicken noodle soup or broth or other family remedies when sick. And by no means am I referencing anointing yourself with olive oil as a symbol of faith in Christ as demonic since Christians understand the olive oil is not the source of power itself. On the contrary, potions you must stay clear of typically include esoteric knowledge—hidden knowledge practiced in secret to influence the outcomes of one's life and the lives of others.

When Rachel hears of her nephew Reuben's return from gathering a bountiful harvest, which included the mandrake plant, her desperation to conceive a child—even if outside of the will of God—caused her to plead with Leah for some of his yield. Rachel's desperation is so great that she enticed Leah by bartering Jacob's presence and body for the night for the plant. Bible Hub's Topical Bible sites the mandrake as an active ingredient utilized in potions and during rites geared toward sexual arousal and fertility.

In Genesis chapter 30, we witness Rachel's growing envy of her sister, Leah, because she is unable to conceive. When Jacob snaps at Rachel because she is distraught over her barrenness, his response points to God as the ultimate source of the blessing of bearing children. Rachel, in her agony, does as Abraham's wife Sara did and tells Jacob to marry and sleep with her handmaiden, Bilhah. When Bilhah bears Jacob two sons, Leah encourages Jacob to marry her maid, Zilpah, and she bears Jacob two sons as well, which spurs Rachel's reckless abandon to get her hands on Reuben's mandrakes.

Genesis 30:1–16 NKJV
"Now when Rachel saw that she bore Jacob no children, Rachel envied her sister, and said to Jacob, 'Give me children, or else I die!' And Jacob's anger was aroused against Rachel, and he said, 'Am I in the place of God, who has withheld from you the fruit of the womb?' So she said, 'Here is my maid Bilhah; go in to her, and she will bear a child on my knees, that I also may have children by her.' Then she gave him Bilhah her maid as wife, and Jacob went in to her. And Bilhah conceived and bore Jacob a son. Then Rachel said, 'God has judged my case; and He has also heard my voice and given me a son.' Therefore she called his name Dan. And Rachel's maid Bilhah conceived again and bore Jacob a second son. Then Rachel said, 'With great wrestlings I have wrestled with my sister, and indeed I have prevailed.' So she called his name Naphtali. When Leah saw that she had stopped bearing, she took Zilpah her maid and gave her to Jacob as wife. And Leah's maid Zilpah bore Jacob a son. Then Leah said, 'A troop comes!' So she called his name Gad. And Leah's maid Zilpah bore Jacob a second son. Then Leah said, 'I am happy, for the daughters will call me blessed.' So she called his name Asher. Now Reuben went in the days of wheat harvest and found mandrakes in the field, and brought them to his mother Leah. Then Rachel said to Leah, 'Please give me some of your son's mandrakes.' But she said to her, 'Is it a small matter that you have taken away my husband? Would you take away my son's

mandrakes also?' And Rachel said, 'Therefore he will lie with you tonight for your son's mandrakes.' When Jacob came out of the field in the evening, Leah went out to meet him and said, 'You must come in to me, for I have surely hired you with my son's mandrakes.' And he lay with her that night."

As unfortunate as it is to read about two women, let alone two sisters, vying over one man, my focus for now is on Rachel's desire for the mandrakes. The mere mention of the plant and its use as an aphrodisiac and fertility aid *(see Blue Letter Bible study guides *mandrakes (D. Guzik, C. Smith)* during these times leads me to logically conclude that Rachel prepared a potion in hopes of becoming pregnant. Her maiden's birth of two sons with Jacob did not satisfy her desire to become a mother. Rachel still desired to give Jacob a child from her own womb—with God or without Him. Yet, we discover that although her desperation was great and put her faith in the mandrakes to end her misery, the plant did not help her conceive.

God's exasperation and anger with Rachel *may* be reflected in His immediate blessing of Leah with three additional children after Rachel's rebellion. We can safely deduce that if indeed the mandrakes would have worked, Rachel's conception would have been cited immediately after she received the plant, yet it is not. Instead, we learn that Leah conceives her fifth and then sixth son and then a daughter. Only after this does the Bible state that **God remembered Rachel** and opened her womb.

Genesis 30:17–24 NKJV
"And God listened to Leah, and she conceived and bore Jacob a fifth son. Leah said, 'God has given me my wages,

because I have given my maid to my husband.' So she called his name Issachar. Then Leah conceived again and bore Jacob a sixth son. And Leah said, 'God has endowed me with a good endowment; now my husband will dwell with me, because I have borne him six sons.' So she called his name Zebulun. Afterward she bore a daughter, and called her name Dinah. Then God remembered Rachel, and God listened to her and opened her womb. And she conceived and bore a son, and said, 'God has taken away my reproach.' So she called his name Joseph, and said, 'The Lord shall add to me another son.'"

Again, as I have previously stated, God is intentional. And His refusal to open Rachel's womb after she so desperately sought mandrakes to create a fertility potion illustrates His desire for our reliance upon Him and Him alone.

Curses (Spells, Hexes and Incantations)

Curses and curse throwing are as prevalent today as they were in biblical times—even if we do not realize it. Many times, when one casts a curse, it is deliberate and directly focused on the desired goal, carried out with steely intention. Other times, curses are laid carelessly without much heed given to the words directed at others. Whether spoken in jest, during arguments, or chanted in passionate repetition with unshakeable resolve, words are powerful and capable of creating prisons of limitation and strongholds of bondage in our lives and in the lives of others. And yes, you can knowingly or unknowingly, intentionally or unintentionally, curse yourself.

Proverbs 18:21 NIV
"Death and life are in the power of the tongue, and those who love it will eat its fruits."

Exposed

Matthew 12:36–37 ESV
"'I tell you, on the day of judgment people will give account for every careless word they speak, for by your words you will be justified, and by your words you will be condemned.'"

If you have ever been in argument and snapped, "You'll always be broke, single, dramatic, angry, overweight…single, alone, no one will ever want you," or the like, you have cursed whoever was on the receiving end of your tirade. Curses in this manner can be just as powerful as someone kneeling over your picture reciting the same in a dark, hypnotically melodic, spine-chilling tone.

Proverbs 12:18 TLV
"There is one whose rash words are like sword thrusts, but the tongue of the wise brings healing."

Proverbs 15:4 NRSV
"A gentle tongue is a tree of life, but perverseness in it breaks the spirit."

Today, throngs of people refute the existence of curses and their power. Yet many of us recently watched a social media reel of a woman pricking a doll made in the image of a prominent athlete during a championship game. Others of us are opening our favorite social media applications today to witness the uproar associated with an accomplished and well-known comedian's appearance on a famous streamer's podcast, where the comedian pronounced death in two years over one of the streamer's close friends. While I don't believe the comedian meant intentional harm, we may never know the impact of those words in the spirit realm—especially if the young man is not a believer in Christ.

The Bible illustrates and alludes to the prevalence of curse casting and its power. In Job 2:9, Job's wife advised him to "Curse God, and die." Weighty words spoken at the height of frustration, hopelessness, and anger with a husband for his refusal to abandon a God she believed had long abandoned him. In Genesis 27:13, in the face of Jacob's fear of stealing Esau's birthright, his mother, Rebekah states, "Let your curse be on me, my son." Again, I implore us to consider King Balak's words to the diviner and prophet Balaam in Numbers 22:6: "Therefore please come at once, curse this people for me, for they are too mighty for me. Perhaps I shall be able to defeat them and drive them out of the land, for I know that he whom you bless is blessed, and he whom you curse is cursed." Do not be misled; curses exist. There are intentional and willful practitioners and careless, unknowing practitioners.

When considering dating in this current day and age, my goal in writing this book is to acquaint you with the hidden dangers of connecting to romantic partners that are not God-ordained for your life and who are spiritually unaware of the times in which we currently live. Further, my aim is to assist you with guarding yourself against those who are aware they are not meant to be in your life but are determined to change that by any means—even if those means are nefarious in nature.

It is paramount that you be particularly mindful of whom you share pictures, intimate belongings, and your handwritten words, as these things can be utilized as touch points to connect with you in spiritual realms during rituals, curses, and spells. You must be careful of whom you allow in your home due to the obvious dangers but also to ensure you are not exposing yourself to a practitioner of the dark arts or someone who is flirting with others who dabble in the dark arts. Again, I am not an expert on the matter, but the Holy Spirit uses me and my experience with an ex to reveal that if someone touches your furniture, clothing, bed, or anything that you have consistent contact with long after they are gone, they can use it to cause spiritual interference, disruption, and harm.

When exploring Samson's entanglement with Delilah for further examination, I discovered that there is a warning for believers that many of us tend to trivialize. Yet, embedded in Delilah's removal of Samson's hair, is a strong admonition. Be very careful to whom you grant access. Access to your body, personal space, possessions, spiritual gifts, and assignments is critical to your ability to survive, thrive, and to flourish as a believer, and they should be handled with vigilant and faithful stewardship. While it is true that Samson's strength lay in his hair—once this secret was divulged to Delilah, it was cut and immediately his covenant position was forfeited—I believe the removal of his hair allowed for the legal operation of curses in his life. Curses that Delilah may have previously cast but which had been ineffective were now able to operate with full efficacy.

Judges 16:19 NKJV
"And she made him sleep upon her knees; and she called for a man, and she caused him to shave off the seven locks of his head; and she began to afflict him, and his strength went from him."

I assert that this affliction was not limited to harassment, mocking, and jeering, but it included curses that previously had no power and had borne no fruit in Samson's life. As such, when dating, entertaining, considering and identifying potential mates, kingdom-ordained and otherwise, partnership with and submission to the Holy Spirit and practical Bible-led wisdom is essential.

Destiny Swapping /Transference
I believe I have been the victim of destiny swapping and transference attempts. And while I don't believe it is common, I believe that there are individuals and groups who firmly believe they can, and will go to great lengths to spiritually attach themselves to a person's destiny. If they are envious, greedy and desperate enough, lustful and prideful men and women will engage in this practice believing it will yield the success, power, and influence they seek. Whether these attempts are physically orchestrated or spiritual rituals done in secret, God's children are becoming increasingly aware of their existence. There are those of us who seek the Lord for prosperity, abundance, healing, protection, and *shalom*, and there are others who can be described as hunters of souls, destinies, and the light in others. I assure you that El-Roi—the God that sees all—is aware, and unless they repent and cease their dalliance with witchcraft, judgment will be righteous, swift, and for eternity.

Ezekiel 13:18 ESV
"And say, 'Thus says the Lord God: Woe to the women who sew magic bands upon all wrists, and make veils for the heads of persons of every stature, in the hunt for souls! Will you hunt down souls belonging to my people and keep your own souls alive?'"

Manipulation (Mental, Emotional, Spiritual, Financial)
The quintessential element required for successful witchcraft endeavors is manipulation. Whether it be emotional, spiritual, psychological, or financial, manipulation is the building

block of most witchcraft efforts. The Cambridge Dictionary defines manipulation as "controlling someone or something to your own advantage, often unfairly or dishonestly." To be clear, manipulation is indeed the cornerstone of intentional and evil bewitching attempts; yet all manipulation, even if one does not believe they are practitioners of witchcraft and sorcery—for example, advocates and students of the popular books rooted in Machiavellian tenets for exercising power over others—are guilty of wielding witchcraft and sorcery. And unfortunately, those who practice do not leave these practices for the business meetings and boardrooms. Many practice these same behaviors in relationships, friendships, and in their marriages.

If we utilize these stories as guides, we discover that there are certain actions and activities that are within the parameters of acceptable behavior to attract one's spouse. Isaac and Rebekah teach us to actively involve the Lord in the process by petitioning Him for guidance and confirmation. Ruth and Boaz teach us to seek godly, respectable mates whose reputations precede them. Jacob and Rachel teach us that when one truly desires us, they will prove themselves to be suitable mates. Even the story of Queen Esther teaches us that a God-ordained mate will honorably commit without triangulating one love interest against another, just as King Ahasuerus chose Esther over Vashti and the other maidens without incident (Esther 2). *Marriage partners that God has chosen will be honorable in their efforts to court us and will love us freely and willingly without us having to resort to manipulative ploys, spells, and witchcraft.* At no time do we ever read of a chant spoken, an oracle summoned, or a potion created or ingested to solidify a God-ordained marriage.

By this we can surmise that witchcraft is particularly abhorred by the Lord—especially when considering some of the reasons for which it is employed. Again, I have not been called to condemn anyone for past actions, but I am called to teach those who want to live within the bounds of what the Lord states is acceptable when searching for, courting, and loving their divinely chosen mates. Many people turn to witchcraft due to natural human desires that we can all relate to, like the need for companionship and affection, while the objectives of others may be downright sinister. Yet, we must remember that there are acceptable ways to achieve love, prosperity, happiness, and protection according to the precepts set by the Kingdom of God and His word, and there are ways that are spiritually illegal and should never be initiated or practiced.

As a rule of caution, I implore you to be especially wary of potential mates, male and female, that were previously gang affiliated, purveyors of narcotics (notorious drug traffickers), or any illicit activities prior to coming to Christ. Many times, under the cloak of secrecy—veiled in clandestine rituals, the wearing of beads and relics, and the choosing of certain tattoos—these individuals have sought protection from those deeply enmeshed in occult practices and beliefs far from God and have often professed oaths and entered into covenants with the demonic. If these individuals have not wholeheartedly repented or successfully completed the deliverance work necessary to break these ties, oaths, and/or covenants, their presence in your life can open doors to chaos, abuse, unrelenting spiritual attacks, and catastrophic loss.

In this journey, we all long for genuine love, companionship, loyalty, support, and the like—yet none of us are perfect. Every relationship will face its share of highs and lows. There will be seasons of unbridled joy with our loved ones, just as there will be seasons of pruning, friction, and refinement. True love and deep intimacy cannot flourish without growth, and growth often demands uncomfortable stretching. Foundationally, as believers, the partners we choose—whether in romance, business, or fellowship—should ultimately reflect the fruits of the Spirit. And if, or when, they do not, with the guidance of the Holy Spirit, we must be honest in our assessment—and just as honest and courageous in our efforts to remove ourselves.

Matthew 7:16 NKJV
"You will know them by their fruits."

Galatians 5:22-23 NKJV
"But the fruit of the Spirit is love, joy, peace, longsuffering, kindness, goodness, faithfulness, gentleness, self-control."

2 Corinthians 6:14
"Do not be unequally yoked together with unbelievers. For what fellowship has righteousness with lawlessness? And what communion has light with darkness?"

CHAPTER 3

Discernment and Dominion

7 Keys of Witchcraft for the Believer:
1. Witchcraft is real
2. Witchcraft in certain hands is powerful
3. The Bible makes no distinction between white and black magic. There are no good, white, or God-pleasing witches. There is no such thing as good and evil witchcraft. Whether you consider yourself a white witch or engage in black magic, God's judgment is the same. The Bible firmly states that it is an abomination unto the Lord (Deuteronomy 18:9-12).
4. Witchcraft is crafty and subtle in its seduction of believers. If it is not in the Bible, or if it is vehemently opposed in the bible, avoid it. As such, the believer should have no dealings with tarot cards or tarot card readers, belief in the zodiac, horoscopes or numerology, the acquiring and harboring of crystals and stones for protection, ancestral worship, good fortune, the burning of sage for protection or to remove negative energy or spirits, candle burning with your intentions inscribed on its body, etc.
A good rule of thumb concerning witchcraft is, "When in doubt, don't."

5. From a spiritual lens, witchcraft holds no legal authority to touch, harm, influence, or impact a believer who has openly confessed and received Yeshua HaMashiach—Jesus the Christ—as Lord and Savior. Once a believer is baptized, covered by the blood of the Lamb slain before the foundations of the world, and actively partakes in the sacrament of Holy Communion, any form of witchcraft becomes spiritually restrained and prohibited from gaining ultimate victory over them. (Isaiah 54:17)

6. Believers who have professed Christ, covered themselves in His blood, take communion and have been baptized, but are intentionally, willfully, and unrepentantly engaged in continual sin (transgressions, abominations, iniquity, and wickedness) are indeed subject to witchcraft and demonic influence. Unrepentant sin—sin which one does not turn away from, hides, or excuses—gives the demonic realm and beings legal ground on which to operate.

7. If one claims to be a believer but does not truly believe in the inherent power within the name of Yeshua HaMashiach and His finished work on the cross, I would surmise that the lack of faith would terminate any protection one might have against witchcraft and leave you woefully susceptible to demonic interference. Saved, but not delivered.

Objectives for Practicing Witchcraft May Include:

- Companionship
- Affection
- Loneliness
- Reversing an unwanted breakup
- To regain access to a loved one
- To keep another in bondage

- Influence
- Secure resources
- Upward mobility
- Worship / Energy
- Co-dependency
- To thwart growth

- Power/Control
- Revenge
- Vengeance
- Jealousy/Envy
- Possessiveness / To end a relationship
- Greed/Avarice

Characteristics of Witchcraft Practitioners:
- Desperate
- Mentally ill/ Delusional
- Lustful
- Broken-hearted
- Naïve and unassuming
- Prideful/Egocentric
- Narcissistic / Energy vampires
- Those who desire worship / slaves, indentured servitude, and opposition to free will
- Con artists/ Swindlers
- The demonically influenced (unknowingly, willingly, and/or intentionally)

Signs a Person Is a Practitioner of Witchcraft or Has Started to Dabble in Witchcraft/The Dark Arts:
- Sudden and excessive deaths in their family
- Sudden change in sexual preferences /openness to sexual perversion, immorality, lewdness
- Sudden change/strong affinity for drugs and alcohol (excessive, addictions)
- Professions of doubt in the God of Israel
- Newfound gods and/or spirituality, and willingness to convert/practice induction rituals
- Hostility toward followers of Christ/Christians
- Admission/allegiance to religions, worship, spirituality that does not profess Christ as Lord, and the open showcasing, attaining, and wearing of jewelry, relics, symbols reflecting their beliefs
- Open reference to themselves as a witch, wiccan, root worker, spiritualist, etc.
- Admission/allegiance to Satan (via explicit profession "demon time," phrases that speak of one's willingness to go to hell, spend eternity in hell, drag another to hell, reciting lyrics that profess allegiance to Satan, promote darkness, sinful lifestyles, and ill-will)
- Sudden inexplicable sickness of the practitioner
- Surrounded by sudden, inexplicable calamity

Outward/External Manifestations of Witchcraft During Season of Attack:
- Dreams/visions of those sending attacks and what is being done in the spirit

- Nightmares/attacks in dreams (assaults, robberies, attacks on loved ones, etc.)
- No fault collisions/car crashes (out of nowhere/side-swiped, hit from behind)
- Emergence of reptiles, insects, vermin, crows, owls (inside household, blocking entryways)
- Inexplicable and cyclical lack and poverty
- Opportunities that disintegrate at the edge of breakthrough
- Rampant betrayal/attacks by loved ones, friends, acquaintances
- Group rejection, (excessive and pervasive), slander, gossip/tarnishing of your reputation
- Stubborn acne breakouts
- Inexplicable and excessive weight gain
- Loss of hair

While many of these manifestations may be considered normal, chalked up to a person's lot in life, or circumstances of a valley season, the best way to gauge whether you are under demonic attack or if a relationship/friendship has opened doors to witchcraft is by seeking the answer from the Lord with prayer and fasting. In addition, ask yourself if the person's presence in your life has caused your life to improve, implode, evolve, or devolve? If that line of questioning does not offer clarity, ask yourself, has their entry into your life stolen your peace? Has your peace and equilibrium been disrupted? Has it remained constant or has it soared to new levels of love, light, joy, service, prosperity, and abundance? Has your relationship with God and His Word grown or has it been stunted? Were you once on fire and passionate about God and have become lukewarm and lethargic regarding His hand in your life and the purposes for which He called you? Often, many of us have a person around us that we know for sure is a man or woman of God, not a self-righteous, judgmental person, but a prayer warrior that you reach out to when prayer or godly wisdom is needed. Consider your relationship with this person; are you still in contact with them or has the relationship become strained and distant? Granted, these are questions you must ask over time as initial contact may be shrouding in attention, affection, and charm. Yet, over time, contact with a person dabbling in the demonic when you are a believer walking with Christ will undoubtedly have a negative impact and influence on your life.

How to Escape a Soul Tie or Emerging Soul Tie with a Witchcraft Practitioner:

- Renounce all allegiance to Satan and to false gods, deities, and darkness
- Rebuke the person, powers, principalities, spirits, souls, etc. attacking you in the name of the Lord
- Plead the Blood of the Lamb over yourself, loved ones, home, possessions, travel, situation, etc.
- Praise the Lord and offer heartfelt adoration and worship daily
- Pray often (set aside specific times each day for prayer and worship, do not waiver)
- Fast often
- Take communion often
- Read the Bible daily

- Gird yourself with the Armor of God (Ephesians 6:10–18)
- End all contact with the person/persons under demonic influence—immediately and entirely
- Forgive your attacker/attackers wholeheartedly and ask the Lord for guidance regarding commencing prayer and intercession for them
- Join/attend a Bible-centered church

Know this with certainty: it is not by our own works that we escape the throes of witchcraft or demonic attack. Yet our worship, praise, honor, and reverence for God—along with our obedience and the posture of our hearts—create the atmosphere for Him to move. These are the very things—the fruit of a true relationship with Him—that invite His intervention, prompting Him to rise against our enemies and fight on our behalf.

Exodus 15: 3 KJV
"The LORD is a man of war: The LORD is His name."

Exodus 14:14 KJV
"The LORD shall fight for you, and ye shall hold your peace."

Deuteronomy 20:4 NKJV
"For the lord your God is He who goes with you, to fight for you against your enemies, to save you."

Denial of the Word of God, the Power of God, and Lack of Knowledge

There are many people that will dismiss this guide as foolishness, poppycock the demented imaginations of a Christian who has gone wild, been indoctrinated with fantasy and fables, and is mentally ill. I would surmise that anyone that identifies as a follower of Christ that is not, at the very least, open to understanding the knowledge contained in this book or others like it, is not acquainted with the Bible or the wisdom therein.

1 Corinthians 1:18 NIV
"For the message of the cross is foolishness to those who are perishing, but to us who are being saved it is the power of God."

1 Corinthians 2:14 NKJV
"But the natural man does not receive the things of the Spirit of God, for they are foolishness to him; nor can he know them, because they are spiritually discerned."

1 Corinthians 10:21 NIV
"You cannot drink the cup of the Lord and the cup of demons too; you cannot have a part in both the Lord's table and the table of demons."

Hosea 4:6 KJV
"My people are destroyed for lack of knowledge."

Yet, as followers of Christ, we must always remember Yeshua HaMashiach's declaration regarding His identity, His mission, and the adversary He identifies—along with that adversary's objective. With spiritual understanding, we discern that Yeshua is simultaneously exposing the persons, beings, entities, voices and ideologies that operate apart from and outside of His authority and in direct opposition to Him—undoubtedly including witchcraft and the occult. He does not merely expose these forces; He also illuminates the choice set before us. Whether we are seeking salvation and understanding, or love, provision, protection, and direction, He alone is both the standard and the solution.

John 10:1-4 NKJV
"Most assuredly, I say to you, he who does not enter the sheepfold by the door, but climbs up some other way, the same is a thief and a robber. But he who enters by the door is the shepherd of the sheep. To him the doorkeeper opens, and the sheep hear his voice; and he calls his own sheep by name and leads them out. And when he brings out his own sheep, he goes before them; and the sheep follow him, for they know his voice."

John 10:7-10 NKJV
"Then Jesus said to them again, "Most assuredly, I say to you, I am the door of the sheep. All who ever came before Me are thieves and robbers, but the sheep did not hear them. I am the door. If anyone enters by Me, he will be saved, and will go in and out and find pasture. <u>*The thief does not come except to steal, and to kill, and to destroy.* I have come that they may have life, and that they may have it more abundantly.</u>"

Matthew 7:26-27 NKJV
"But everyone who hears these sayings of Mine, and does not do them, will be like a foolish man who built his house on the sand: and the rain descended, the floods came, and the winds blew and beat on that house; and it fell. And great was its fall."

Matthew 7:21-23 NKJV
"Not everyone who says to Me, 'Lord, Lord,' shall enter the kingdom of heaven, but he who does the will of My Father in heaven. Many will say to Me in that day, 'Lord,

Lord, have we not prophesied in Your name, cast out demons in Your name, and done many wonders in Your name?' And then I will declare to them, 'I never knew you; depart from Me, you who practice lawlessness!"

CHAPTER 4
Witchcraft's Vessel: Architect of Deception and Demonic Assault

In my previous book, *The 7:47 Connection: Called to a Higher Altitude*, I detailed how Satan and the kingdom of darkness attack and hunt believers through society's pervasive narcissistic culture; narcissistic people make it woefully easy for Satan to persecute, oppress, and oftentimes seduce believers to abandon God. I have taken the liberty of including many of these revelations below for your knowledge, protection, and ultimate victory.

25 Characteristics of the Narcissistic Experience
1. Unspoken and secret telepathic communication
2. Degradation of you—your looks, intelligence, destiny, etc., marked as humor
3. Abuse (mental, emotional, physical, financial, sexual or hyper-sexual activity), etc.
4. Inability for perpetrator to sincerely apologize
5. Forced sleep deprivation
6. Baseless accusations/fabricated drama

7. Smear campaigns/Gossip and slander
8. Slow, methodical chiseling away of your resources
9. Gaslighting
10. Enjoyment from your pain/exacting cruelty upon target
11. Gang stalking (recruitment of others to monitor, surveil, intimidate, mock, and/or jeer you)
12. Silence as a weapon
13. Cyclical abandonment
14. Inability to take accountability
15. Excessive drug and/or alcohol abuse
16. Violent tirades and/or explosive physical attacks
17. Triangulation (setting you against their old and/or new romantic partners, proteges, friends, and family members to feign innocence, blamelessness, and/or victimhood)
18. Inability to make lasting change
19. Expectations of savior-like love and loyalty/insatiable demands that they cannot and will not reciprocate
20. Trouncing of boundaries (personal, privacy, violation/manipulation of electronic accounts and devices)
21. Plans to "unalive" you
22. Intentional damage of property
23. Hiding and/or stealing of personal property
24. Utilization of masks before your family and loved ones to appear genuine, mild-mannered, and loving

followed by eventual theft of these relationships (the Narcissist replaces you)

25. Fake tears/contrived emotions

Bonus

Grandiose proclamations of superiority/ God complex (comments regarding their deity made in gist, but secretly and deeply believed)

Intense rage disproportionate to the offense

⚠ **If indeed your involvement with the Narcissist does not include many, if not all of the aforementioned elements, you undoubtedly acknowledge and realize a seemingly irreversible, irretrievable waste of your time and resources.** Here the word, "seemingly" is utilized intentionally because this feeling and experience of loss can be redeemed, and you can and will be restored by Yeshua HaMashiach.

⚠ **The Narcissist is cloaked with a mantle of disloyalty and deception geared toward your pain and humiliation**

5 Stages of Narcissistic Abuse through a Spiritual Lens:
1. Love bombing and bewitchment (*Future Faking)
2. Consummation of soul tie (usually through fornication or adultery)
3. Verbal and sexual hypnosis
4. Bondage and imprisonment
5. Your spiritual and/or physical death

5 Elements of Spiritual Death by the Hand of the Narcissist:
1. Catatonic, fog-like state or trance

2. Demonic theft/hemorrhaging of natural and spiritual resources
3. Destiny alteration (the stealing of your star, unconscionable delay, unrealized divine purpose)
4. Your separation from the love and presence of God (idol worship)

⚠ The hidden, yet Ultimate Goals of the Narcissist:

1. Total eradication and obliteration of your divine inheritance
2. Total eradication and obliteration of your commitment and desire to fulfill your purpose and diving calling at the appointed time

⚠ Eventual Fate of the Narcissist:

1. Exposure that galvanizes a grievous existence leading to true, unwavering repentance
2. Exposure that galvanizes a grievous existence leading to eternal damnation

⚠ Ways in Which Demonic Spirits are Transferred/Ways That Allow for Legal Operation of the Demonic:

1. Sexual activity (*fornication/*adultery)
2. Close repeated proximity
3. Music (negative, violent, blasphemous, repeated exposure)
4. Video footage (repeated exposure to negative, violent, blasphemous, cinema, television, video games, music videos, etc.)

5. Declarations and decrees (intentional and careless)
6. Bloodline/Generational curses
7. Drug/Alcohol abuse
8. *Idolatry (Worship of/excessive devotion to another other than the One True Living God)

Important Keys to Remember:
⚠ Payment or requests to a known practitioner of the dark arts to spiritually harm, vex, hex, delay, monitor, or sabotage another is witchcraft. It is dabbling in the occult, a portal to the demonic and a demonic covenant legalized through the exchange of tender via your financial resources or unperceived vow of loyalty.

⚠ The Narcissist is a wolf in sheep's clothing and will resort to the dark arts—black magic, witchcraft, star/destiny tracking, tarot cards, sorcery, hexes, vexes, spells, incantations, sex, and demon worship to keep you bound and trapped in trauma.

⚠ The spell-casting Narcissist has been relegated to a reprobate mind and is stuck in a state of perpetual reverse, "backwardness" and/or illogical decision making.

⚠ The spell-casting Narcissist hunts the children of God but eventually attracts their own kind as a secondary supply source (the child of God is their primary/ideal source). Spiritual attacks from the Narcissist, their secondary supply/supplies, and the coven of witches and warlocks to which they have pledged allegiance to—knowingly or unknowingly—is not uncommon. Watch for attacks from people that you have had no specific or direct contact with but who target you to demonstrate their loyalty to the Narcissist. Be mindful that the attacks show up as malignant, widespread group think when considering the disdain for you that pervades the group, community, and/or organization.

⚠ **The Narcissist is not a hunter of empaths. The Narcissist is a demonic hunter and spiritual predator; they are an agent of darkness and dispatched assassin on assignment to target and take out the prophets and children of God—even when they themselves do not realize how they are being used.**

The Stages out of Narcissistic Abuse to Spiritual Wholeness:
1. Escape
2. Survival (excessive spiritual warfare and retaliation during this phase)
3. Readjustment (excessive spiritual warfare and retaliation during this phase)
4. Healing (lightbulb moments/ instances of clarity that reorganize memories/incidents)
5. Restoration
6. Testimony

When you are the target of witchcraft and you are walking with Christ in sincerity, repentance, and obedience, you may not feel the full force of the attack. Yet you will still discern and experience the interference of demonic activity. To what extent, I cannot predict, for it is intricately tied to God's will in the matter, the measure of your faith, your spiritual understanding and preparedness, and your willingness to both stand firmly on God's Word and actively engage in spiritual warfare.

Psalm 144:1 NKJV
"Blessed be the LORD my Rock, who trains my hands for war, And my fingers for battle—"

Ephesians 6:12 NLT
"For we are not fighting against flesh-and-blood enemies, but against evil rulers and authorities of the unseen world, against mighty powers in this dark world, and against evil spirits in the heavenly places."

However, I also understand that the battle belongs to God. When you are His child, no matter what happens, how it may look, how it started, or is currently going, God will have the victory.

Isaiah 54:17 KJV
"No weapon that is formed against thee shall prosper; and every tongue that shall rise against thee in judgment thou shall condemn. This is the heritage of the servants of the Lord, and their righteousness is of me, saith the Lord."

The weapons form, the attacks and strikes may land, but ultimately, they fizzle, flounder, and fail. When attacks are allowed to flourish for a season, I surmise the Holy Spirit allows this for several reasons. The first is to make the believer aware of what's being done against them. The second is a warning for believers to set themselves apart and to let go of habits, relationships, or influences that may endanger their well-being or threaten their spiritual walk. And the last is God's intent to use your attack as a demonstration to practitioners that He alone is the one true and living God—omniscient, omnipresent, and omnipotent. When people choose to attack God's children, servants, and prophets, there will be repercussions. He will not stand by idly. He will allow an appointed time for repentance. However, after that window closes, I assure you that sickness, death, and destruction immediately follow.

1 Chronicles 16:22 KJV
"Touch not mine anointed and do my prophets no harm."

Psalm 105:15 NKJV
"Do not touch my anointed ones and do my prophets no harm."

Micah 5:12 NIV
"I will destroy your witchcraft, and you will no longer cast spells."

KJV
"And I will cut off witchcrafts out of thine hand; and thou shalt have no more soothsayers."

ISV
"I will render your witchcraft powerless, and mediums will no longer exist among you."

⚠️ **The only true victory over the Narcissist is to profess, confess, and truly surrender your life to Yeshua HaMashiach, Jesus Christ, the Son of the Living God.**

In the same way, the only true victory over—and freedom from—witchcraft, oppression, and every form of demonic assault is found in the love, light, and merciful arms of Yeshua HaMashiach. He was, He is, and He will forever remain the triumphant One—the eternal answer and unrivaled victor over Satan and every force of darkness.

Matthew 28:18 NKJV
"And Jesus came and spoke to them, saying, 'All authority has been given to Me in heaven and on earth.'"

John 3:35
"The Father loves the Son and has placed everything in his hands."

John 5:22 AMP
"For the Father judges no one, but has given all judgment [that is, the prerogative of judging] to the Son [placing it entirely into His hands]."

1 Corinthians 15:24–28 ESV
"Then comes the end, when he delivers the kingdom to God the Father after destroying every rule and every authority and power. For he must reign until he has put all his enemies under his feet. The last enemy to be destroyed is death. For "God has put all things in subjection under his feet." But when it says, "all things are put in subjection," it is plain that he is excepted who put all things in subjection under him. 28When all things are subjected to him, then the Son himself will also be subjected to him who put all things in subjection under him, that God may be all in all."."

If you have not accepted Jesus Christ as your Lord and Savior, or if you believe in your heart that you have lost your way and want to return home, His love and forgiveness is always available to you—and the heavens have been awaiting your return home.

Luke 15:10 NKJV
"Likewise, I say to you, there is joy in the presence of the angels of God over one sinner who repents."

CHAPTER 5

Freedom in Christ

Invitation to Follow Christ and Share in the Gift of Salvation

If you desire to break free from all forms of witchcraft—whether you have been a victim, an agent, or an enabler—and return to the love of God, experiencing His peace, joy, victory, and healing in this life, and securing eternal life with Him as a partaker of His grace, mercy, presence, and kingdom in the life to come, then I implore you to speak the words below aloud, believing them deeply in your heart:

Father God, I believe you are the creator of heaven and the earth, the heavens above the heavens—everything therein, and everything there below.

I believe John 3:16 that states, "For God so loved the world that he gave his only begotten son that whomsoever believes in Him shall not perish but have everlasting life."

Lord God, I believe your son, Yeshua HaMashiach, Jesus the Christ, was conceived by the Holy Spirit,

Born of the Virgin Mary,

Suffered under Pontious Pilate, was crucified, died, and was buried

And on the third day, He rose again.

He ascended into heaven and is seated at the right hand of God the Father Almighty,

creator of heaven and earth.

I believe He will come again to judge the living and the dead.

Father God, I repent for my sins, known and unknown, intentional and unintentional,

And I ask your forgiveness.

I invite your Son to come into my heart and my life

I submit to Him fully and wholeheartedly and declare Him as my Lord and Savior.

I petition you Father God, according to thy will and by and through the power of the Holy Spirit

for Yeshua's blood to wash me clean,

and I thank you for a new heart, a new spirit, and a renewed mind.

In the Mighty, Matchless, Majestic name of Yeshua HaMashiach, Jesus the Christ,

Son of the Living God,

The Righteous Advocate,

The Messiah and Savior of the entire world,

Amen.

You are now a blood-bought child of the Most High God and a follower of Christ—redeemed, forgiven, and saved. I encourage you to find a Bible-based church and Christ-centered community as you begin your journey to walk in the love, light, faith, and authority of our Lord and Savior, Yeshua HaMashiach, Jesus the Christ. May He guard and guide you as you love others, speak the truth in love, and shine your light wherever darkness and deception attempt to prevail.

www.ingramcontent.com/pod-product-compliance
Lightning Source LLC
Chambersburg PA
CBHW040422100526
44589CB00021B/2793